Switzerland

Occupying 41,000 sq km (16,000 sq miles) of Central Europe, Switzerland comprises the most mountainous landscapes in the continent. Bound in by France, West Germany, Austria and Italy, this landlocked republic has had to fight long and hard to maintain its proud traditions of independence and neutrality.

Today Switzerland is a modern and technologically advanced nation that boasts one of the highest standards of living in the world. Famous historically for its banking system, it has now developed important chemical and instrument-making industries. The country's industrial base is to a large extent founded on its long tradition of craftsmanship, which still survives in the form of woodcarving and watchmaking.

Although Switzerland is an advanced industrial nation, it still offers some of the most beautiful scenery in Europe. Spectacular Alpine landscapes blend with verdant pastures and the snow-capped mountains offer a wide variety of winter sports. As a result, the people of Switzerland – who are descended from Germans, French, Italians and others – reap the benefits of a healthy tourist industry.

In *We live in Switzerland* a cross section of Swiss people – young and old – tell you what life is like in their country; in the cities and the mountains, in industry, in school and at home.

Preben Kristensen is a widely traveled freelance photographer and Fiona Cameron has written a number of books for children, including *We live in Belgium and Luxembourg* and *We live in the Netherlands*.

we live in
SWITZERLAND

Fiona Cameron
and
Preben Kristensen

The Bookwright Press
New York · 1987

Living Here

We live in Argentina
We live in Australia
We live in Belgium and Luxembourg
We live in Brazil
We live in Britain
We live in Canada
We live in the Caribbean
We live in Chile
We live in China
We live in Denmark
We live in East Germany
We live in Egypt
We live in France
We live in Greece
We live in Hong Kong
We live in India
We live in Indonesia
We live in Ireland
We live in Israel
We live in Italy

We live in Japan
We live in Kenya
We live in Malaysia and Singapore
We live in Mexico
We live in the Netherlands
We live in New Zealand
We live in Pakistan
We live in the Philippines
We live in Poland
We live in Portugal
We live in Saudi Arabia
We live in South Africa
We live in Spain
We live in Sweden
We live in Switzerland
We live in the U.S.A.
We live in the Asian U.S.S.R.
We live in the European U.S.S.R.
We live in West Germany

First published in the
United States in 1987 by
The Bookwright Press
387 Park Avenue South
New York. NY 10016

ISBN 0–531–18090–5
Library of Congress Catolog Card Number: 86–62099

First published in 1986 by
Wayland (Publishers) Ltd
61 Western Road, Hove
East Sussex BN3 1JD, England

© Copyright 1986 Wayland (Publishers) Ltd

Phototypeset by Kalligraphics Ltd
Redhill, Surrey
Printed in Italy by G. Canale & C.S.p.A., Turin

Contents

"There are few women in banking with responsible jobs"

37-year-old Margrit Huser is the manager of a branch of the Union Bank of Switzerland (UBS), one of the world's largest banks. She has worked at UBS in Zurich for fourteen years.

I have been very lucky – there are very few women in banking with responsible jobs. What's more, I didn't plan my career – it just happened! I started in 1972 as a secretary in the training department, with three girls under me. In 1975 I was made the head of training programs in the commercial department of UBS and stayed there for nine years. UBS puts a lot of emphasis on training all of their staff so it was a great responsibility. At first it

It is important for people to get on well together in an open-plan office.

was difficult to work on my own because I'd always had a boss before who would decide everything for me. But it was challenging and interesting and I learned how to deal with people.

It was interesting being in the head office of a bank like UBS, because there were a lot of creative people and I felt at the center of an important industry. Switzerland has always been an important banking center for many reasons, including its political stability and banking secrecy regulations. UBS handles investments for people from all over the world and plays an important part in the Swiss economy, with about 280 branches in Switzerland alone.

In 1984 I had the opportunity to do a training program myself and was sent to France and England to improve my languages. When I returned I was made the manager of this branch in Zurich with twenty-one people working under me.

It's a small, open-plan branch, so everyone has to get on well together for it to work. I think that it's just as important

At the central dealing room of UBS in Zurich stocks and shares from all over the world are bought and sold.

to be a good manager as it is to be a good banker, because you have to create a good atmosphere to make people happy in their work. Most of the time we handle cash transactions as we get a lot of passing trade, but we also deal with some private investments involving bonds, shares and foreign exchange.

I'm also studying for an MBA in my spare time. I have classes two evenings a week and on Saturday mornings. It's a lot of work, but I feel it's necessary to develop my skills. If I were to start my career again, I would study economics or law first in order to have a better foundation for the banking world.

When I'm not working or studying, I like to read and play a little golf. It's not always easy to combine personal and working goals. I would only get married if I found someone who was prepared to fit in with my career.

"Quartz changed our lives"

Marcel Jeanbourguin, 52, is a watchmaker and lives in La Chaud De Fonds. He works for Ebel, a family business that specializes in high quality watches.

My father was a watchmaker, and from the age of four I would spend all my time in his workshop. He had his own business with eighteen watchmakers and himself assembling the pieces. I never wanted to be anything else – everyone who was anyone in this town was a watchmaker.

When I left school, I was advised to be a shoemaker, but I refused and went instead to the technical college to do a four-and-a-half year apprenticeship as a

Watchmaking requires a keen eye and a great deal of patience.

watchmaker. I had to learn about mechanics, tools and how to make the pieces. My uncle was a professor there and so he would always give me the most difficult pieces to make. My father gave me a bench in his workshop, so I got a lot of practice and eventually finished second in my class.

I then went to work with my father. I worked there, assembling watches, for twenty-three years. In the 1950s and 60s, there was a boom and we couldn't produce enough.

But then the recession came in the mid-1970s and the advent of quartz meant that accurate watches could be produced easily and cheaply. The Japanese flooded the market with cheap watches and that hit us very badly. Quartz changed our lives. In the past it had required great skill to achieve precision and suddenly that skill was no longer required. A watch that had contained two-hundred pieces now contained only twenty.

La Chaud De Fonds was the cradle of the watchmaking industry in Switzerland. It all started and developed here. But by 1979 there was no more work. My father's workshop closed down and I had to find something else to do.

Ebel is a small company run on American lines, specializing in only the highest quality goods. They turned watchmaking into an assembly line, where workers were taught only one part of the watchmaking process, but they also needed someone who could do everything, so they took me on.

Now, out of 250 employees, only fifteen are watchmakers, but they still need us to repair broken or damaged watches. Ebel is among the few watchmaking companies that are doing well. That's partly because of marketing and partly because

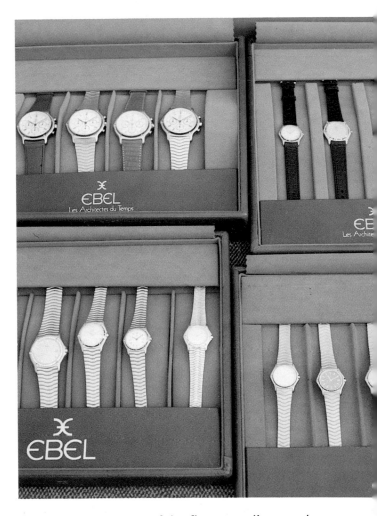

Ebel produces some of the finest quality watches in the world.

we still produce the best. Another area that is beginning to pick up is the very cheap range of watches, such as the Swatch, which provides a good lesson for everyone in marketing techniques.

But La Chaud De Fonds has had to change. Of the nine people who finished in my class, only five are still working as watchmakers. My two sons both wanted to become watchmakers, but I told them to go into electronics instead. It is interesting that we choose to diversify into other high precision industries – it must be in our blood.

"The biggest piece we ever made weighed 100 tons"

Bruno Kübler, 49, works as a meister (foreman) in the foundry at Georg Fisher AG in Schaffhausen. It is Switzerland's biggest metal foundry.

My family has always lived in Schaffhausen, which is a beautiful, historical city with 34,000 inhabitants. It is a very peaceful place and is situated close to the Rhine Falls, which is the biggest waterfall in Europe.

I have been working in the foundry of Georg Fisher AG for twenty-four years. My father also worked here for thirty years before he retired, so you could say that it's a family tradition. I started as an unskilled worker because mine is the kind of job that you can't learn purely by theory – you have to have practical experience and start from the bottom. After about four years of learning you finally get to work on the furnaces. I took a further education course provided by the firm and learned a lot about different metals and their properties in various alloys. After two years of studying, I was made a foreman. I worked as a foreman for thirteen years before I was made a meister. My job now consists of preparing and supervising all the processes leading to the casting. We produce around seventy different kinds of alloys, but our biggest sales are in steel alloys. GF, as the company is called, is a multi-

Most of the production process is regulated from the central control room.

national company, with 16,000 employees and subsidiaries in many countries producing a whole range of different products.

In the big foundry all our products are made to order from drawings. We start by creating the form in sand, then the metal is melted and the exact alloy mixed. Steel changes its physical properties with the amounts of carbon, chrome, nickel and other substances you mix into it. One of the biggest pieces we ever made here at GF, was a water-turbine wheel weighing 100 tons. It was made of chromo-nickelsteel in a special alloy in order to create a strong, hard, but still flexible, corrosion-resistant metal.

The metal is melted in up to four different melting pots. Heat is generated to bring the metal up to 1,680°C (3,084°F). Several samples are taken to be analyzed by our laboratory to ensure that all the right ingredients are present in the right quantities and that there are no impurities.

When the liquid steel is ready, and its temperature has fallen slightly to 1,580–1,600°C (2,900°F–2,940°F), it is poured into the sand form and left to cool, which for some of the big pieces can take up to fourteen days. After the form has been taken away, it is often necessary to heat up the piece and cool it very slowly several times to remove tensions in the metal, which inevitably occur during the casting. It is often only these final, very carefully conducted, heating and cooling processes that create the perfect piece of metal with the exact properties that the client wanted us to produce.

It's a hot job inspecting the preheating of the big melting pots.

"We produce 1,600 million kWh per year"

48-year-old Georges Dayer is an electrical engineer working for the Grande-Dixence S.A., the company responsible for the production of hydroelectric power from the waters of the Grande-Dixence Dam, in the Alps south of Sion.

Hydroelectricity is the most important source of energy in Switzerland, although nuclear power is gradually taking a larger share (currently about 30 percent of the total). The Grande-Dixence is Switzerland's largest hydroelectric development and it contains the world's highest dam. The scheme uses not only water from the valley of the Dix, where the dam is situated, but also meltwater from thirty-five glaciers in a catchment area that stretches from the Mischabels to Mont Blanc and from Zermatt to Arolla. Since some of these are lower than the dam the waters are first collected and then driven up by four pumping stations through tunnels into the lake. On a map it looks as if the water is defying gravity! The total volume of water diverted in an average year by this system is about 420 m³ (111 billion gallons). Sometimes there are problems when an installation is actually covered by a glacier. There are

The turbines in the Chandolin power station are driven by the waters of the Grande-Dixence Dam.

still some aspects of nature that continue to defy man!

Most of the water is collected in the summer. The Grande-Dixence Reservoir has a storage capacity of 400 million m³ (105 billion gallons). The dam looks small next to the mountains, but it's 285 m (935 ft) high and 198 m (649 ft) at its widest point, big enough to hide the pyramids and several cathedrals! Inside the dam, there are 32 km (20 miles) of galleries and pipes, containing control instruments. A tunnel supplies water from the reservoir to two power stations: Fionnay and Nendaz, which produce an average of 1.6 billion kWh per year, distributed to industries and households in seventeen cantons. The bulk of this production takes place in winter when most of the electricity is required. The dam is only accessible by helicopter during the winter, so

The Grande-Dixence Dam is the highest in the world.

workmen and technicians go there only when necessary, which is usually about once a month.

I was born in this valley and my father was also a hydroelectric engineer. I've been working here for twenty years. I'm responsible for the surveillance of all the computerized installations and for the best exploitation of the electricity produced. Much of this is also determined by computers.

One of the nice things about hydroelectric power is the feeling that it is clean. The dam itself and the reservoir have become huge tourist attractions, while the power and pumping stations have been built largely underground.

13

"Everything is written in two languages"

Inge Margot teaches German in the bilingual community of Biel, which lies at the foot of the Jura mountains. Biel marks the dividing line between the French- and German-speaking areas of Switzerland.

Switzerland has four national languages: German, French, Italian and Romansh. The majority speak German, while French is spoken mainly in the southwest and west, Italian in the south and Romansh (by a very small minority) in the east. In fact the situation is more complicated than this because a great many dialects of each language are also spoken in different places. The German-speaking Swiss, in particular, have many variations of Schweizerdeutsch, which is itself a dialect and quite different from the written Hochdeutsche, which is taught in schools. Hochdeutsche is used mainly for official and business purposes.

Biel is on the border between the French- and German-speaking regions and is the only officially bilingual community in Switzerland. This means that everything is written in both languages

Even the road signs in Biel are written in German and French.

including official documents and such things as street signs and advertisements. We even have a bilingual newspaper, where all the articles and even the cartoons are written in both languages.

Language isn't just a matter of communication – it's also an expression of cultural background. We try to teach people about their own cultural heritage, while appreciating that of others. Thus parents have the right to decide whether to send their children to a French- or German-speaking school. The classes will be taught in one language and will have a cultural bias, but in the fourth year the other language will be taught very intensively, so all the inhabitants here are bilingual. I could ask someone a question in German and be answered in French and I probably wouldn't even notice.

As there are more German- than French-speaking people, all foreign children are sent to the French schools. This is also because most of the foreigners are Italian and find French easier than German. There is a great cultural mix here and because everyone has friends speaking another language, they make more of an effort to understand each other.

That isn't to say that there aren't any problems. For one thing, it's more difficult for the French, because they get used to hearing and speaking Schweizerdeutsch, but then have to learn Hochdeutsche, which they have no opportunity to practice. For another, the mentalities of the different groups are different, but this is a problem that concerns the country as a whole. As the majority of the Swiss speak German, they are in a position to pass laws that aren't necessarily to the liking of those speaking French. The Germans tend to prefer to regulate things more than the French, who prefer to leave things alone.

Biel is full of colorful and unusual statues.

15

"Schools here don't provide lunch"

13-year-old Ursula Bühlmann lives with her family in Lucerne and goes to the Mariahilf, one of the oldest secondary schools in the city.

My father is a truck driver and my mother is a housewife. I am the youngest of five children. We live in a small block of apartments with five other families in the old part of Lucerne. It takes me about fifteen minutes to walk to school, though in the summer I go by bicycle.

I'm in the second year of the Mariahilf secondary school. It has about 250 pupils altogether, with eighteen to twenty girls and boys in each class. All the schools here are mixed. I have classes in German, French, math, biology, history, geography, gymnastics, painting, religion and handicrafts. I like German and French best. Lucerne is in the German-speaking part of Switzerland, but we have to learn French in the secondary school. I have thirty lessons a week from Monday to Saturday, starting at 7:45 am and going on until 4:30 or 5:00 pm, with Wednesday and Saturday afternoons free and two-and-a-half hours lunch-break. The schools here don't provide lunch so everyone goes home. Most people live nearby so it isn't a problem, but it's not so nice for those whose mothers are at work all day.

I have about an hour's homework each day, so I don't have much free time. But

All the schools in Switzerland are mixed.

I like reading adventure novels and watching television. I also belong to a youth organization for girls, which meets every second week. It organizes games and cheap vacations in the mountains in the summer. Most of the girls in my class belong to it and the vacations are fun, but I find that the meetings take up too much time and are rather boring, so I'm thinking of giving them up.

The education system in Switzerland is rather complicated because every canton has its own school system with different rules and regulations. Only certain aspects are decided by the country as a whole. In Lucerne, everyone has to go to school for a total of nine years, usually from seven to sixteen. Like most people I went to kindergarten for two years first. After primary school there is a test and then you go either to a secondary school, like me, or to a cantonal school. Secondary school lasts for three years, after which you get a school report, whereas the cantonal school lasts for six or seven years and ends with the Matura exam, which is set by the Swiss Federation. You have to pass the Matura in order to go to college. So in a way your fate is decided after elementary school because it would be difficult and expensive after normal secondary school for most people to study for the Matura exam, although theoretically it's possible.

I shall leave school when I'm sixteen but I don't know what I shall do then. Most people go to a technical or commercial school, or become an apprentice for three years in a firm, combining theory with practical experience. The only thing I do know is that I'd like to work with young children, perhaps in a kindergarten.

The Kapellbrucke was built in the fourteeth century and has become a symbol of Lucerne.

"The Swiss produce 10 percent of the world's medical drugs"

Bringfried Tschanz-Hungerbühler, 51, is a chemical worker at the pharmaceutical company of F. Hoffmann-La Roche in Basle. He has been with the company for thirty-six years, producing "active substances" in medicines.

I joined the pharmaceutical industry when I was fifteen years old because everyone said that this was where the future lay. I must admit that they were right, and now I wouldn't work with anything else or for anyone else. Our working day here at La Roche starts at 7:00 am and lasts until 4:07 pm – not a minute less, not a minute more. This is the famous Swiss punctuality for you.

F. Hoffmann-La Roche forms a large part

A lot of research into new drugs is carried out by scientists at Hoffmann-La Roche.

Bringfried makes the final adjustments to the machinery before it is switched on.

of the industrious Swiss chemical industry, which exports goods worth around fourteen billion Swiss francs each year. This is one-fifth of the total Swiss exports. Yet the chemical industry employs only one-tenth of the total Swiss workforce. The production is mostly concentrated on pharmaceutical products (40–45 percent) and dyestuffs, mostly for textiles. It is an interesting fact that the Swiss produce 10 percent of the world's drug requirements, 13 percent of its dyestuffs and 20 percent of its perfumes and flavorings.

There are lots of reasons for Switzerland's growth in the chemical industry. One is that we don't have very many raw materials ourselves and therefore we must make products in which labor accounts for a large proportion of the value added. Another is that chemical plants are very expensive to establish. In Switzerland capital for this is readily available. Finally, the workforce in the chemical industry has to be very highly trained and specialized. The Swiss workforce meets these requirements.

F. Hoffmann-La Roche produces lots of different drugs. The most well known of these is probably Valium, a tranquilizing drug, used for nervous disorders. However, we also produce a whole range of vitamins, antibiotics, painkillers and hormones. We have produced antimalaria pills for many years and lately production has just started on a new one, called Lariam, which has been developed in cooperation with the World Health Organization. Apart from all this we also produce a large amount of liquid crystals, which play an increasing role in displays in watches, calculators, instruments and portable computer screens.

The company looks after its workers extremely well. We have the biggest company sports club in Switzerland, comprising a sports hall, swimming pool and a soccer field among other things. However, now that I am over fifty, I'm content to stick with my hobbies, which are cross-country skiing, cycling and the vegetable garden.

"There aren't as many woodcarvers as there used to be"

Fritz Fuchs-Stähli, 43, is a woodcarver. He lives and works in Brienz, a small town on Lake Brienz in the canton of Berne. He is married and has two children.

Most people in Brienz are farmers. Woodcarving developed as a hobby – it was something to do during the long winters when the fields were covered with snow. People started decorating their houses, which were all made of wood, and then their tools and then they started carving figures.

Brienz is close to Interlaken, which began to develop as a center for tourism

Fritz produces a wide variety of wooden figures.

in the early 1800s. Tourists started buying carvings to take home as souvenirs and gradually woodcarving developed as a major industry in Brienz. Someone set up a factory to organize it and in 1884 a wood-carving school was built, which is still the only school for woodcarving in Switzerland. Gradually, it became for many people a full-time occupation, instead of being just a hobby.

My father was a farmer, but he used to carve wooden bears as well. Bears are popular souvenirs, because the bear is the symbol of the canton of Berne. There's a bear pit, which is a major tourist attraction, in the city of Berne, so they were easy to sell. I used to help my father in his workshop at home when I was twelve years old. Later, when I left school at sixteen, I became an apprentice at Huggler-Wys, the largest woodcarving company in Switzerland. I'm still working here twenty-seven years later, although I'm now the manager. It's a family business with sixteen woodcarvers and has both a factory and a shop with a workroom, so that visitors can see how we work.

I see myself as a commercial sculptor and craftsman rather than an artist, although I have made some special sculptures for an exhibition. Most of the pieces are made in linden wood, which comes from this area. It is light in color, soft but still firm and doesn't crack, so it is nice to work with. I also use harder woods from nut trees, cherry trees, pear trees and maples for some special pieces. The wood is aged for about two years before being worked.

We work from traditional prototypes but also develop new designs and variations and do special pieces on commission. Some of the most popular items are nativity crib scenes – we sell about 10,000 every year! My brother also works here. He specializes in animal figures, while I specialize in figurines. Between us we are training two apprentices.

There aren't as many woodcarvers here as there used to be – there is competition from cheaper, machine-made imports and there is less money in it than there is in other jobs. But there will always be a niche for a good craftsman because there will always be people who want something made by traditional methods. It's a nice way of life for someone who's calm and patient and likes working with his hands.

Fritz is often commissioned to carve religious statues for churches.

21

"Saas Fee is a carless town"

Reinhold Supersaxo, 39, is a hotelier, ski instructor and mountaineer in the tourist resort, Saas Fee. He has studied music and plays several traditional Swiss instruments, among them the enormous alphorn.

I have few regrets in my life, one of them, however, is that I never took the mountain guide exam. I was too busy studying music and when I finished, it was too late; you have to take the exam before the age of twenty-five. Nevertheless, I have climbed all the important peaks, the Matterhorn, Mont Blanc, Monte Rosa and Grand Combin to mention a few. I have even made movies about them. Here in Saas Fee we have the highest Swiss mountain, Dom, which reaches 4,545 m (14,900 ft).

I started climbing and skiing when I was about five years old. My father, who was also a mountain guide, took over the old Alphubel Hotel, which was built by my grandfather. We used to have lots of English people coming here to climb. They would always take a mountain guide along and in those days, until the late 1950s, there were just under one hundred professional mountain guides in the village. Today, there are only about twenty; most people nowadays prefer to climb on their own.

Reinhold plays the famous Swiss alphorn for the tourists who stay in his hotel.

It takes great skill to play the cowbells!

Saas Fee has 1,120 inhabitants, but in the high season, like Christmas vacations, it swells to about 10,000. The town is basically run by nine families and as a visitor you see these names again and again; Bumann, Supersaxo, Zurbruggen, Burgener, Andermatten, Anthamatten, Kalbermatten, Lomatten and Imseng. We own fifty-six hotels and forty-five restaurants among us.

There are many reasons for Saas Fee's popularity as a tourist resort; we have the most fantastic scenery at our doorstep, which provides a perfect setting for winter sports, summer walks and mountain climbing. We have developed all the necessary facilities. On top of this, Saas Fee is a carless town; you have to leave your car outside the city. The only means of transportation are a few silent, electrical "taxis" or walking. Our climate is exceptionally good, with a very high proportion of sunny days.

My hotel, the Alphubel, has eighty beds in forty-one rooms. We belong to a club of Swiss hotels that have decided to supply extra facilities for families with children. We have a kindergarten and special rooms with an adjoining children's room. Furthermore, we arrange lots of entertainment and excursions that include activities for the children, such as alphorn blowing contests.

Although I should not complain, my life as a hotelier is a bit dull, I really would have preferred to be a mountain guide!

"Basle is the home of the Swiss merchant navy"

56-year-old Hans Wegmüller has worked in the port of Basle for twenty-eight years. He is a manager at one of the port workshops but loves to build model railroads in his spare time.

I live in Basle, which is the second biggest city in Switzerland, with a population of 200,000. It is situated 273 m (895 ft) above sea level and is divided into two parts, Great Basle and Lesser Basle, by the 265 m (870 ft) wide river, the Rhine. Basle is the home of the Swiss merchant navy.

The commercially navigable Rhine begins here and ends in Rotterdam. A promontory in the river, called "Dreilandereck," (the Three-Countries Corner), is where the three nations, France, West Germany and Switzerland meet. It is also a meeting place for barge people from numerous countries. Basle is linked to Rotterdam by a regular steamer service and is the home port for some 500 river-going vessels. The fact that the Swiss federal customs authorities collect half their total customs revenues in Basle alone, underlines its enormous importance as a shipping center. More than one-third of Swiss foreign trade is transported on the Rhine, Switzerland's only direct link to the sea. The first steamship arrived in Basle in 1832 and a direct steamship connection to London was established in 1844. Today, passenger ships still undertake the four-to-six day journey on the Rhine to Rotterdam.

The big crane has a lifting capacity of 50 tons. It loads the railcars directly through the removeable roof.

24

I work for a company called Birs, which is situated in Birfeldenhafen, one of Basle's four harbors. Our main activity is the loading, unloading, storage and transportation of some of the 12 million tons of the various goods that are handled in the ports each year. We do a lot of transportation door-to-door, and we are even able to transport specially heavy or bulky items up to about 1,000 tons in weight, which cannot be transported by rail or road. For this purpose we can use our roll-on/roll-off ships, which can take the goods directly to Scandinavia. The newly constructed container terminal in Birfeldenhafen has a capacity of 30,000 containers per year.

I have worked for Birs for twenty-eight years. After training as a machine mechanic, I worked for some years as a crane driver. Now I am managing the

Goods that should not be exposed to bad weather are stored in a huge warehouse.

workshop; you have to be able to do a little bit of everything when you are working for a firm that has only thirty-five employees.

In Switzerland you do not have to be a member of a worker's union, and only, about fifty percent of the people employed in the ports are members. I guess this is partly due to the fact that our salaries are very high and there is generally a good relationship between the workers and the management. Just after World War I there was a very serious general strike that damaged the country's economy – no one is interested in a repetition.

My work is in shifts from Monday to Friday but I sometimes have to work on weekends, for which I am paid overtime. When I finish my work for the day, I always look forward to getting home to my hobby, which is building model railroads. I have one model that covers an area of 8 sq m (26 sq ft) in one of the rooms in our house!

"You can't wear high heels as a geologist"

Anne-Marie Bruttin, 35, obtained a degree in geology from the University of Lausanne last year and now works for a consulting firm of engineers and geologists.

Only five women have ever graduated from Lausanne's Institute of Geology and two of those are now married, have children and don't work! I suppose that it's not a very feminine profession. I spend my life in jeans and boots – no high heels or nail polish! It's very much a male environment and difficult for a woman to break into, especially as there aren't many jobs around. I was lucky because I started working part-time for this firm while I was still studying, so they knew my work and offered me a full-time job when I graduated.

I've always enjoyed the outdoor life – my father had a construction business and I was always fascinated by the problems involved in building. I prefer working to studying – I'm continually learning something new and it's more satisfying to be doing practical work. It's hard financially to go to college in Switzerland – there are very few scholarships available and they provide only the minimum amount required for survival.

The course at Lausanne covered a very wide range of topics including geology, physics, chemistry and minerology as well as a lot of field work.

The Institute of Geology in Lausanne has thousands of rock samples.

Here I'm more specialized. We do a lot of work for both private industry and government bodies. We also do quite a lot of hydrology. If, for example, a highway is to be built, we look into the water resources of the area and make proposals for their protection. We also control the pollution levels in the water and check the waste put out by factories, to make sure they're not above the levels laid down by the law. The Swiss are becoming more and more concerned about the environment.

We also do work for construction companies, reporting on the underlying soils and rocks to determine how the foundations should be laid. A lot of our work involves drilling in the area concerned.

Both the geology and hydrology of Switzerland are complex. Switzerland forms part of the Alpine arc that stretches almost 1,000 km (600 miles) from Nice in France, to Vienna in Austria. The Alps make up the southern two-thirds of the country, while the central plateau and the Jura mountains make up the rest. Switzerland also forms part of the three main continental river basins. Over two-thirds of the country is drained via the Rhine into the North Sea, while about 27 percent is drained by the Rhône, the Po and the Adige into the Mediterranean. Four percent flows via the Inn into the Danube and eventually into the Black Sea.

The beautiful city of Lausanne is situated on the shores of Lake Geneva.

"The highest railroad station in Europe"

62-year-old Hans Kellerhals is a railroad engineer. He has been working in the Jungfrau region of the Bernese Oberland for the last thirty-eight years.

As in most European countries, the railroads were developed first by private enterprises in Switzerland at the end of the nineteenth century. But Switzerland had particular problems, with its mountainous landscape, so special railroads, called rack railroads, were adopted to deal with the steep gradients. One of the most spectacular of these is the Jungfrau railroad, which reaches the Jungfraujoch. At 3,454 m (11,333 ft) this is the highest railroad station in Europe. The railroad itself is 9 km (6 miles) long, with a gauge of 100 cms (39 inches) and gradients of up to 25 percent.

It took Hans twelve years to become a first-grade railroad engineer.

The Federal Railroad was created in 1898 after the purchase of five of the independent lines and electrification of the system began in 1899. Some of the main train tunnels were constructed around this time: the St. Gotthard in 1882, the Simplon in 1906 and the Lötschberg in 1913. All of these were major feats in engineering and helped to open Switzerland up to international traffic. But there are still about 2,000 km (1,242 miles) of private lines carrying about one-third of the total number of train passengers carried each year.

I always wanted to be a railroad engineer, but I spent several years as a mechanic first, before moving to Zweilütschinen, near Interlaken. Then I joined the Bernese Oberland Railroads (BOB) when I was twenty-four years old. The BOB was opened in 1890 and runs trains from Interlaken Ost to Lauterbrunnen and Grindelwald. It used to be completely private, but now the State has a stake in it.

Hans used to help maintain the trains but now he only drives them.

The total length of the railroad is 23 km (14 miles). There are gradients on my route of up to 12 percent and the gauge is 100 cm (39 inches). In winter it can be difficult to keep the tracks free of snow. It's always quite busy because of the skiers in winter and climbers and walkers in summer.

It took me about twelve years to become a first-grade engineer. Now I work for eight hours a day and have 116 days vacation per year. The countryside is so beautiful that I never get tired of the route, although the variations in the times when I work can make life difficult sometimes. Until I reached the age of fifty-eight, I had to do maintenance work on the trains as well as drive them, but now I only have to do the driving. I get a lot of spare time and like precision shooting and stamp collecting. The best thing about retiring when I'm sixty-five will be the fact that I won't have to look at my watch any more!

"It took ten years to make the St. Gotthard road tunnel"

Arturo Schatzmann, 51, is a civil engineer. He has been working for an engineering firm, Electrowatt, in Zurich for twenty-five years and was project manager of the St. Gotthard road tunnel, which is 16 km (10 miles) long and one of the longest road tunnels in the world.

Civil engineering is a fascinating job because it is very varied and can cover all sorts of areas like hydroelectric power stations, roads and bridges. But for me, tunnel engineering has been the most interesting of all because it combines structural and rock surveys, geology, electrical knowledge, technology and managerial skills.

Heavy machinery is used to drill the holes for the explosives and to take away the loose rock.

In the 1960s and 70s, life was exciting because Switzerland was investing a lot in their communications network, especially in roads and railroads. I worked on the St. Bernardino tunnel, which is 7 km (4 miles) long, and then the St. Gotthard tunnel, from the early project stages, right through to the end. It isn't so easy now because people are more concerned about the environment and feel that enough construction work has been done.

In the twelfth century, a mule track was established over the St. Gotthard pass because it was the shortest route between northwestern and southern Europe, but it was always a difficult route. In 1882, a railroad tunnel was opened, which was eventually able to carry cars. But this still wasn't enough to provide for the mounting traffic, so in the 1960s it was finally decided to build a highway and a road tunnel. The tunnel would go from Göschenen in the Canton of Uri to Airolo in the Canton of Ticino.

A competition was held for suitable projects, and the list was narrowed to two from a group of sixteen. Electrowatt won the project on the basis of cost. The basic design had four ventilation shafts and included a parallel safety tunnel.

It was a great experience working on the site; I had to coordinate between the two cantons, Uri, which is German-speaking and Ticino, which is Italian-speaking. As I was brought up in Ticino I am almost bilingual. Most of the three hundred construction workers came from Italy, so we had to provide housing and other amenities for them. Unfortunately, because of space and cost, we were not able to to let their families come too.

The work was divided in two, starting at the tunnel portals of Göschenen and Airolo in the autumn of 1969. Blasting

Laser beams were used to ensure that the tunnel was being built in a straight line.

bores were drilled at the tunnel face and filled with explosives, a round was blasted and the material was then removed. The safety tunnel was excavated simultaneously.

In some ways our lives were made easier because the train tunnel was nearby, so we knew what to expect. We also had the most modern technology available and were able to use lasers in between the formal surveys to make sure that we were going straight.

But there were some areas that were very difficult. We had to go through many different types of rock: granite, sedimentary rocks (limestones, shales, marbles and sandstones), through to the crystalline mantle of the Gotthard Massif and slate. The sedimentary areas were particularly difficult as they were much softer and needed to be supported to prevent their caving in. It took ten years to make the tunnel and it was a great moment when, on December 16, 1976, the two teams met in the middle. The tunnel was finally opened in 1980.

31

"There has been a surge in violent crime"

34-year-old Fritz Diethelm is a policeman in the town of St. Gallen. He works for the Statt Polizei in the motor traffic department and drives a patrol car in the winter and a motorcycle in the summer.

To become a policeman in Switzerland you first have to have learned a trade. I was originally a cook, working in the eastern part of the country but my military service interrupted this. When I finished I had to look for a new job. I thought, "Why not try something different?" and applied for a job with the police. I passed the tests, which consist of examinations in arithmetic, dictation and geography, together with some psychological and physical tests. Having passed these, you have a year of schooling, which includes both theoretical and practical work. The basic training culminates in taking the oath and swearing to obey the Swiss laws.

A police officer's work is very interesting, but it also puts quite a strain on normal family life as it consists of both day and night work.

Our police station here in St. Gallen is quite small and we look after a jail with thirty-five cells, which contain people who are awaiting trial. The police in Switzerland are divided into two main categories: Canton Polizei and Statt Polizei. The latter take care of the towns and the former take care of the countryside, investigate unsolved crimes and take over cases after the Statt Polizei have made an arrest and are pressing criminal charges.

The traffic in St. Gallen is constantly surveyed by eleven television cameras.

Fritz often checks the motors on mopeds, which are restricted to a top speed of 30 kph.

I belong to the Statt Polizei, which maintain the law in the cities. When we arrest a criminal or are called to a crime, we write a report about it. From then on, the case is taken over by the Canton Polizei, who investigate it further and bring any resulting charges to the courts.

My work is actually in the traffic patrol, and consists of making sure that the traffic laws and regulations are kept. This covers a broad spectrum of things: from checking that truck drivers don't drive for more than nine hours per day, to speed control with radar or measuring the alcohol level in a driver's blood.

In the cold Swiss winter we patrol in cars, but in the summers we use BMW motorcycles. We have lots of trouble with young people who make illegal changes on their mopeds in order to make them run faster than the 30 kph (19 mph) permitted by the law.

Switzerland used to be a very peaceful little country inhabited by law-abiding citizens, but during the last few decades we have felt the surge in violent crime that other countries are experiencing. The number of violent attacks and narcotic crimes have also become big problems here. Many youngsters are riding their motorcycles and snatching bags from elderly ladies. Gas stations and taxi drivers are also more frequently robbed than when I started as a policeman thirteen years ago.

"This is a small community, protected by high mountains"

Father Burgener, 50, is a Roman Catholic priest, who lives and works in the town of Saas Fee in the canton of Valais. As well as conducting the Mass he spends much of his time visiting the old and the sick.

Almost everyone in this area is Catholic, although in Switzerland as a whole, the numbers of Catholics and Protestants are roughly equal, with small minorities of other religions. Switzerland has always been a magnet for refugees, such as the protestant Huguenots in the sixteenth century and more recently, Muslims from Sri Lanka. People here have complete

Father Bergener's mass in Saas Fee attracts a large congregation.

freedom in religious matters. People weren't always so tolerant. Switzerland was torn apart by religious wars during the Reformation and Counter-Reformation. In fact, disputes over religious questions very nearly prevented the creation of the Swiss Federation.

The cantons of Fribourg and Valais were never really affected by the Reformation and have always been almost entirely Catholic. I was born in Zermatt, in the next village from Saas Fee and was brought up as a Catholic. I wanted to be a priest from a young age, like my older brother, who also became one. I don't think one chooses to become a priest — one is chosen by God and must follow that calling. So I studied at the universities of Fribourg and Innsbruck, which were very international and stimulating.

The population here is swelled by the huge numbers of tourists. In the winter, they only want to ski and have nothing else on their minds, but the summer walkers tend to be more thoughtful and often come to services. I conduct a Mass every weekday morning and hold four Masses on Sundays.

Apart from conducting Mass and spending time in prayer, I visit the old and the sick, either at home or in the hospital and I go to the local schools to teach the children their catechism. It is up to the parents to decide on their children's religious education, but Catholics are under a moral obligation to bring their children up in the Catholic faith.

Like many others in the Alps, Zermatt and Saas Fee are mountain villages, small communities still protected by the high mountains that surround them. But they have changed a great deal in the last thirty years. In the past, the people here were poor and tried to scrape a living from

Saas Fee is a small town but its population is swelled by large numbers of tourists.

the land, with only a small tourist trade. But with improved communications, many villages have become important tourist resorts all year round. There is both work and money. That is good in some respects, but unfortunately, the more material success and wealth people have, the less they seem to feel the need for religion. What they forget is that they can't take it with them when they die. Of course the same thing is happening in the cities too. Sometimes I find it difficult to deal with this sort of mentality.

"Many plants have disappeared or become rare"

Catherine Lambelet, 29, obtained a degree in Agricultural Science and is currently doing research for a doctorate at the botanical gardens in Geneva.

Botanical gardens originated from monastery cloisters where monks grew herbs for medicinal purposes. Later, people started collecting different types of plants and began to analyze and describe them. The botanic garden in Geneva was founded in 1817. Nowadays, it has several purposes: as a place for the scientific study of plants, the development of new species and for

Catherine tends to the plants in one of the green-houses at the botanical garden.

the protection of rare plants. There is also a recreation area to give people a feeling for nature and the countryside. It is used for educational purposes and excursions into the countryside are organized every year, to teach people more about their environment.

I'm working on a project to determine the effects of agriculture on the flora of the fields. Some plants have disappeared or become more rare, while others have increased – they are usually the ones, like grasses, that farmers don't like!

The flora in Switzerland is extremely complex (with about 3,000 different species) because the climate here is so varied. Its central position in Europe means that Switzerland's weather is influenced by the four main European air currents – from the Atlantic, the eastern continent, the northern subpolar region and the Mediterranean to the south. These factors, together with the fact that the relief changes suddenly from mountain to plateau, give rise to many local and regional microclimates. Rainfall also varies greatly from region to region, for example, while Monte Generoso has about 20,600 mm (81 inches) per year, Sion only

Some of the botanical specialize in cultivating Alpine flowers.

has about 5,900 mm (23 inches). So it is impossible to give a description of the Swiss climate in general, except to say that it is temperate on the Central Plateau (average rainfall 100 cm – 40 inches, average sunshine 1,700 hours and average annual temperature 7–9°C, 44–48°F). Otherwise it varies from region to region, depending on such factors as altitude and exposure to wind and sunshine.

The Alps make up about two-thirds of the country and contain some very unusual and rare plants, many of which are protected by law. We have a very good collection of these at the Botanic Garden, which specializes in rockeries, with examples from about 115 different geographical groups, including the Himalayas and China. They are very difficult to grow and require a lot of protection. One of the main problems is protecting them from frost. In their natural habitat, they are protected by a mass of snow during the winter. It may sound odd, but the temperature under the snow never goes below freezing point.

"Skiing is my life"

Michel Datwyler, 39, works as a ski instructor and owns a sports shop in Villars. He was a member of the Swiss national team for many years and skied for Switzerland in the Winter Olympic Games together with his brother.

I was born in Bretaye which is situated 1,800 m (5,904 ft) above sea level and 500 m (1,640 ft) above one of the most beautiful Swiss tourist resorts, Villars. My parents owned a little restaurant where the funicular ends so there were always a lot of tourists around. I started to ski as soon as I could walk and by the time I started school I was already a very good skier. My brother and I would ski down the mountain every morning in the winter and come back by the funicular. Sometimes, when the weather and the snow conditions were right, we would be able to do the downward trip in two or three minutes. But there were times when the loose snow would reach our chests and then it could take up to two hours.

In Villars we have up to six months of snow every year so it is the perfect place for a skiing vacation. I am now the director of the local ski school, director of the association of ski instructors and member of the technical committee of the Swiss ski schools. So, one can easily say that

Many of the ski slopes in Villars run right down to the edge of the town.

Michel teaches hundreds of people to ski every year.

skiing has been, and still is my life. I also own a sports shop in Villars, which of course specializes in ski equipment.

In the period from 1958–60, I skied for the Swiss national junior team. After that from 1962–73 I was on the national "A" team. I used to do all the different disciplines but the one that was always my favorite was the downhill. I guess skiing downhill to school every morning had a lot to do with it.

The area around Villars has numerous downhill runs and lots of ski lifts, funiculars and cablecars to get the skiers up the mountains without too much effort. The downhill runs come in all categories: easy, intermediate, difficult and cross-country. The area also has glaciers, which can be used for skiing even during summer. The rule of thumb is that the temperature falls 1°C (34°F) for every 200 m (656 ft) of altitude. So, if you are 3,000 m (9,840 ft) above sea level, the temperature will be approximately 15°C (59°F) lower than it would be at sea level.

One of the reasons I gave up competing at international level was that I had two serious falls in 1973. I have never broken any limbs skiing, which is quite unusual, but when you fall seriously twice you have to stop and think.

Skiing has improved enormously since I was a child. The equipment produced today is extremely good and anyone can learn to ski in a relatively short time. Around fifty to sixty percent of the people who come to our ski school are beginners and nearly all of them can be let loose on their own after only a week of schooling.

39

"The cows fight to become queen of the Alps"

Lucie Chevrier, 55, lives in Evolène in the Herens Valley. Her life revolves around the annual move of the cattle from their stalls up to the alpine pastures, where they spend the summer months.

In the winter, from about the middle of October until the end of June, the cows are kept in barns in the village. As soon as the weather is good enough and there is sufficient pasture in the fields, we move them up to the Alps. The move is in two

Lucie and her husband take their favorite cow out of the barn for the first time after the winter.

stages. First, we take them up to an intermediate pasture for fifteen days, to give them a chance to acclimatize and then we take them up to the high mountain pastures, which are at about 2,000 m (6,562 ft). We do the same on the way back at the end of the summer. Everyone has a chalet on the intermediate pasture.

When the cows go to the high pastures they are left in the hands of a few men and the rest of us return to the village, to cut the grass and make hay to provide winter feed for the cattle. Most people here own about 1,200 cattle altogether and there are ten or twelve Alpine pastures. About four men are hired to look after the cattle in each pasture: one to clean, one to milk and make cheese and two to look after the cattle.

In the past, everyone made his own cheese, but then the farmers got together to form a cooperative and built a dairy. In the winter the dairy sends a truck around to all the proprietors to collect the milk — about 4,000 liters (1,000 gal) a day. In the summer, things are different. People still do most of the cheesemaking by hand, but a pipe carries the milk down from the pastures to the dairy.

We have very special cows here, which are so well known for their aggressive nature that a sport has been created for them. When people took their cows up on to the pastures after the winter, these cows, or "queens" as they are called, would start to fight each other, by chasing or pushing each other with their horns to determine which was the strongest – the queen of them all for the season. They still do this but now every year the top two hundred of these cows are entered into a cantonal competition and thousands of people watch the finals! People breed

The cow fighting contest is a very popular event in Valais.

them specially and they change hands for about twice the price of any other cow.

The two most important things for a queen to have are a good heritage (from another queen and an aggressive bull) and good horns. Prospective buyers often come to see the movement of the cattle to the pastures. They like to see the younger cows fight in order to judge whether they will make good fighters. My husband has bred several, although he tends to sell them quite early in their careers as he doen't like the risk involved. If they do badly in a season or break a horn, they lose their value very quickly.

Things have changed a lot here. Many people are involved in the tourist industry and aren't interested in dairy farming any more. In 1954, only one person in the village owned a car, but now some people even have two!

"Politics are complicated in Switzerland"

Ruth Geiser-Im Obersteg, 65, fought hard for a woman's right to vote in Switzerland. She was the first woman to be elected to the Executive Council of the City of Berne in 1970, where she worked for the next fourteen years.

Politics are complicated in Switzerland, because it is a federation, made up of twenty-six independent and autonomous cantons and half-cantons. Every canton (and, indeed, certain communes within them) has its own constitution and laws. The duties of the federal government are

The Bundeshaus in Berne is the seat of the Swiss federal government.

laid down in the Constitution of 1848: it ensures internal and external security and maintains diplomatic relations with foreign powers. It controls such things as energy and communications, customs, postal, telegraphic and telecommunications services, the armed forces and creates laws that are fair to all and deals with questions of economic development and social welfare.

The constitution requires government at federal and cantonal level to take the form of a direct democracy. The Federal State consists of the people and the cantons, the Federal Assembly (or Parliament), the Federal Council (or Government) and the Federal Tribunal. Any change in the constitution must be approved by the people, who may also initiate change.

It is strange that it has taken so long for women's rights to be recognized in a country that is extremely proud of its democratic process. We are still very much behind the rest of the Western world in that respect.

I got into politics by accident. My father and my husband were both in the Swiss People's Party (the SVP) and so I became interested in politics. In 1964, I started working in the Association for the Right to Vote for Women. Although women were only given the right to vote in federal matters in 1971, they had been given the right to vote in some cantons and communes before this date and were finally given this right in Berne in 1968. I was the first woman to be elected councilor on the Executive Council of the City of Berne in 1970.

At first I was supported by my party, but they wanted to manipulate me. I was made director of public works, responsible for such things as construction, roads, public buildings, bridges, the zoo, and water purification. It was fascinating, but men hadn't expected me to be doing what they considered to be a man's job — they thought I should be involved in the arts or social welfare. It was unthinkable that a woman should be responsible for public works and everyone was just waiting for me to make a mistake. I had to be perfectly correct in everything I did. My party began to turn against me because they thought I was too independent. I was forced to leave the SVP because of this prejudice in 1976.

However, I was reelected twice with the support of a women's action group. I hope that I have done something to help women. There never used to be any women politicans but now both the town clerk and the president's assistant are women and there are more and more female lawyers. People thought that they would satisfy women's demands by giving them the right to vote, but that was just the beginning.

As the director of public works, Ruth was responsible for the maintenance of many of Berne's important buildings.

"We must be prepared for anything"

Hubert Vuarnoz, 39, is a ferryboat captain working for the CGN, which has seventeen boats on Lake Geneva. He lives with his family in Lausanne, on the north bank of the lake.

My grandfather, my father and I were all born and bred in Ouchy, in Lausanne — what place could be nicer? It has all the amenities of a city, but you can be skiing within an hour. In summer you can do any water sport you like, from sailing and windsurfing to swimming and having fun in a pedalo. Also, the sheer magnificence of its setting, overlooking the lake and the Alps is unbeatable.

I got involved with boats almost by accident. My father was a cabinetmaker and I trained as a decorator and upholsterer. The company that owns all the ferryboats here, CGN, needed someone to refurbish their old boats. They have a lot of modern diesel boats but they also keep about four steamboats. These were built at the turn of the century, and they try to keep them in their original condition. I started refurbishing them in the winter and during the summer, began to work on the boats. I started as a deckhand, then became a ticket collector. I gradually worked my way up to become a captain, taking all the neces-

It took Hubert many years to work his way up from deckhand to captain of his own boat.

sary exams as well as getting practical experience.

The CGN runs many different services including cruises around Lake Geneva. But most of these run only in the summer when the tourists are here. Lake Geneva is about 90 km (56 miles) long and up to 12 km (7 miles) wide. Most of the lake is in Switzerland, but the southern coast, from Hermance in the west to St. Gingolph in the east is in France.

I usually work on the service from Lausanne on the north bank to Evian-les-bains, in France, on the south bank. This service runs all year round, mainly because there are a lot of people who live in France, but come to Lausanne to work. I suppose about six hundred people commute across the lake every day. The journey takes about half-an-hour and is quicker than going by car. In the evening, a lot of Swiss people like going across to the casino in Evian, where gambling is much freer than in Switzerland. The first service starts at 4:30 am and the last one leaves Evian just after midnight on the weekend.

It may seem a short and easy route, but we have to be prepared for anything. The weather can change within minutes, so the boats are well equipped with everything from radar and radio to telephone links. We go through periodic safety-drills and even have contact with a helicopter service if we need it. Ferries have occasionally saved dinghy sailors who have been surprised by very bad weather.

We work very long hours in the summer, but have an extra vacation in the winter, which suits me as I love to go skiing. All the boat maintenance and renovation happens in the quiet season and I still deal with the refurbishing. I like the variety.

Many of the old boats on Lake Geneva have been restored to their former glory.

"Nowadays people prefer fruit, fresh cream and yoghurt"

Christine Buser, 19, is an apprentice pastry chef at Eichenberger, one of the best and most famous pastry shops in Berne. When she finishes her training she will go home to work in her father's bakery in Kirchberg.

My father is a baker and I wanted to become one too, I also wanted to have the best training possible. Eichenberger has a very good reputation and so I came here as an apprentice after I left secondary school. I go to a cooking school every Monday to learn about different types of baking products and then I work here from Tuesday to Saturday, from 7:00 am until 6:00 pm, with two hours off for lunch. Altogether, I do forty-four hours per week,

Christine puts the finishing touches to some elaborate cakes.

the maximum allowed by the unions. The busiest times are at Christmas and Easter, when it's traditional to give confectionery presents to friends and family.

There are about fifty people working here altogether, with different departments for pastries and cakes, puff pastry and chocolate. I have spent six months in each but prefer making cakes. The worst part of the training was learning to make puff pastry, as I had to start at 2:00 am so that all the croissants would be ready by breakfast time. I've been here for almost three years now and finally finish my apprenticeship next month, when I shall also take my final exams at the school. Then I shall get a diploma. After that I go back to work with my father in the family bakery in Kirchberg, just outside Berne.

Switzerland is famous for its chocolates and pastries and the Swiss like them as much as anyone else. We only use the finest chocolate available to make special candy with fruit, cream, alcohol or nuts. Apart from huge quantities of chocolate and sugar, we use about 280 liters (297 quarts) of fresh cream and 200 kg (440 lb)

The store in Berne where Christine works is always full of customers.

of butter every week! Perhaps it's because we produce so much of these products in Switzerland that we had to find a way of using them.

Swiss habits are changing – many old recipes include a lot of buttercream and rich and complicated mixtures. But nowadays people prefer to have more fruit, fresh cream and yoghurt. What they forget is that the calories are the same! I don't have the time to put on weight. We use highly perishable ingredients so we have to make everything fresh every day. It's a lot of work, especially since one is always standing up. When I first started working here, I used to like sweet things, but not any more!

I've been living at home and commuting to work. I haven't had time for any hobbies and whenever I'm not working I have to study for my exams. I'm looking forward to finishing so that I can have more time to myself.

47

"Fifty years ago, every family owned a loom"

Julienne Beytrison, 67, produces handwoven cloth in a small workshop in the village of Evolène in the Herens Valley. Her husband, sister and brother-in-law also work there.

I was born in this village, have always lived here and when I die they will bury me here too! My father worked on the land like everyone else, looking after dairy cattle, cutting the hay and so on. Everything was done by hand. There were eight of us children, four girls and then four boys. We went to school in the winter for six months (every day with no breaks for Christmas or Easter) and then helped with the animals or the hay throughout the summer. Everything was done by hand and it was hard work.

When I was a child, fifty years ago, every family owned a small loom and made all its own material for clothes, curtains and tablecloths. Of course the looms were much smaller than the one I use now, but they were sufficient for people's needs. Hardly anyone knows how to use a loom any more and people don't make their own clothes. There's a couturier here who makes the traditional costumes and a milliner who makes the hats but people go to the towns to buy their other clothes.

Julienne has been producing handwoven cloth since she was a child.

Using a wooden loom Julienne can weave 5m (16 ft) of cloth in a day.

I used to help my mother and then started selling my cloth to others and eventually began working here, thirty-seven years ago. It's the only place producing handwoven cloth in the whole village. I met my husband here – we've been married for thirty-six years. He works here too, carding the thread and looking after all the equipment. My sister and brother-in-law also work here and we all have a good time while we work. My nephew and his family own a store in the village, where the cloth is sold.

Most of my cloth is sold to the tourists now as it costs too much for the local people. That's because the materials have become very expensive. The linen thread comes from Belgium and costs the earth, while cotton is imported into the German-speaking part of Switzerland. Wool is bought locally, but we spin it ourselves. I usually weave cloth with a mixture of cotton, linen and wool so that there is a nice combination of textures. I can weave about 4–5 m (13–16 ft) a day, depending on the design. Some of the designs are traditional, but others come out of my head.

My husband and I both have pensions but we like to do something with our time. When I'm not working here, I like to knit – I can't keep my hands still!

49

"An interpreter must have a quick mind"

Marie-Odile Sigg, 36, has traveled all over the world in her job as a simultaneous interpreter at the European headquarters of the United Nations in Geneva. Her mother tongue is French, but she also speaks German, Italian, English, Spanish and Portuguese.

As a child, I traveled all over the world because my father was a diplomat. I also learned several languages. My mother tongue is French, but I also speak German, Italian, English, Spanish and Portuguese. I wanted to use my languages and continue traveling, so interpreting was the perfect answer. I got a degree in translating before

During a conference Marie sits in a booth and uses the headphones and microphone for simultaneous translation.

going on to study interpreting for another eighteen months at the postgraduate school in Geneva, which is said to be one of the best in the world.

I joined the United Nations in 1975 and spent three years at their headquarters in New York, before coming to their European headquarters here in Geneva.

The United Nations was set up in 1945 to promote peace and cooperation throughout the world and to promote such ideals as equality and basic human rights. It is made up of a number of different councils and agencies, many of which are represented in Geneva. There are now 159 countries that are members and it provides a forum for discussion on political, social and economic issues. Switzerland is one of the few countries that is not a member, because it has always felt that its neutrality might be undermined if it were to join.

There are about 3,900 international civil servants working permanently at the United Nations in Geneva. Simultaneous interpretation into the official languages of the United Nations (Arabic, English, Chinese, Spanish, French and Russian) is provided at about 4,000 conferences a year. So it's not surprising that there are about 250 interpreters working here. A simultaneous interpreter will always

The United Nations European headquarters are based in Geneva.

translate from a foreign language into his or her own language.

I usually do two three-hour stints per day, always working with another interpreter, so that each of us interprets for alternate half-hours. Sometimes I may have to work during the night, I never know until the last minute. The hours are irregular, so it's not for the nervous. You have to have a quick mind and be adaptable. Personally, I like it.

Interpreting requires total concentration and a great deal of general knowledge. It's not enough to simply translate from one language to another. An interpreter must convey a message, the essence of what is being said. It's a heavy responsibility. One must have a cultural background and a sense of history because the work here comes out of the history of this century. One must also follow newspapers and international events and understand the major religions of the world. But it's also stimulating as one can go from talking about disarmament to shipping to commodities to human rights and I often get to travel to conferences being held in other countries.

"Geneva is famous for its cuisine"

Eliane Bouilloux runs the Restaurant Du Vieux-Moulin in Geneva, with her husband Gerhard. It is said to be one of the best restaurants in Switzerland.

I was born in Fribourg, but moved to Geneva when I was five years old and have lived here ever since. When I left school, I worked in a bank for a few years. I met and married Gerhard seventeen years ago when I was in my early twenties. He is French but trained as a chef in Geneva.

After three years of marriage, we managed to buy a café-restaurant in the center of Geneva. I gave up my banking career to work with him and I've never regretted it.

It is important to keep the restaurant's kitchen spotless and well-ordered.

We worked hard and the restaurant was successful but we wanted something bigger. We eventually found the Vieux-Moulin ten years ago. It is situated on the outskirts of Geneva and consists of both a house and a restaurant. We changed the decor completely to give it a good atmosphere and it has worked.

To be a good restaurateur, you must love the work, because it takes up your life, even though we are closed two days a week. We both love it. We have a lot of contact with our clients and many come regularly and have become friends. We've also met a lot of famous people including well-known politicians, sports people, actors and singers.

Gerhard gets up early to go to market and spends the morning preparing food for the day. We have twelve people working for us here, including one apprentice chef, but there's always a lot to do. We are open for both lunch and dinner and are almost always full for the latter. Gerhard takes care of the food, while I take care of the clients. I greet them and take their orders and am there at the end of their meals. I also deal with the money and do all the books – my banking background has come in very useful.

We never have more than thirty-five people here at any one time. This means that we can give a much more personal service than a larger restaurant. That's very important. It's not enough to provide good food and wine – there must also be a good atmosphere and a pleasant and personal service. Small details, such as table and flower arrangements must be perfect.

Geneva is famous for its cuisine – my husband says that it's because of the number of French chefs here! Food plays an important part generally in the lives of the French-speaking Swiss. But apart from

Eliane and Gerhard have deliberately kept the restaurant small so that they can offer a more personal service.

that, Geneva is also rather special, because it is such an important international and cosmopolitan city and it has to cater to a wide variety of tastes.

We make an effort to provide both good and imaginative dishes, such as fish fillets in a shrimp and caviar sauce, scallops in a lime sauce or duck's liver in cider vinegar. Of course, we must always use only the freshest and best ingredients. People like much lighter food than in the past, so we are constantly experimenting with new ideas.

When we're working, we eat very simple food, before our clients arrive. But when we're not working, we love to go out to eat. Even on vacation, we like to find good restaurants wherever we are – it's a major part of our lives.

"Each year about twenty-six people are killed by avalanches"

Professor Claude Jaccard, 57, has been director of the Institute for Snow and Avalanche Research since 1980. This is situated at 2,668m (8,742 ft) above sea level on the mountain, Weissfluhjoch, near Davos.

Here on Weissfluhjoch we study the snow and its various properties so that we can warn the public about the possibility of avalanches. Each year an average of about

In order to study the ice crystal the temperature in the cold laboratory must be kept at −40°C.

twenty-six people are killed in the Swiss Alps by avalanches. Nearly all of these are tourists who didn't respect the warnings issued by us or who went into restricted areas. The number of tourist victims has doubled over the last forty years, but if you consider that the total number of tourists visiting the Alps has multiplied by one hundred in the same period, it is still a very small number.

Avalanches can be divided into two main categories: flow avalanches and powder avalanches, depending on the way they move. A flow avalanche will move downward, over the ground, at a speed of between 60 and 200 kph (37 and 124 mph). A powder avalanche will move faster, from 100 to 300 kph (62 to 186 mph) as a big snow cloud in the air. It is very difficult and rare for even very good skiers to outrun an avalanche if they find themselves in its path.

Our institute is situated in Davos 2,668 m (8,742ft) above sea level, and controls a further seventy measuring stations spread

The institute is 670 m above sea level and commands beautiful views of the surrounding valleys.

out all over the Swiss Alps at altitudes of between 1,000 and 2,500 m (3,280 and 8,200 ft). All the information they gather is relayed to us, and on the basis of the snow's consistency, the temperature and the weather conditions, we then issue an avalanche warning report. We do this throughout the winter season, every Friday and on other days when the situation changes. If the new snow layer is more than 30 cm (12 in) thick there is a danger for tourists. If it exceeds 60 cm (24 in) there is a danger to road traffic and if it is more than 90 cm (36 in) there is a danger for buildings and villages.

But often warnings aren't enough: if there's danger that an avalanche will occur in a certain area, we will often force it to happen under control. This can be done with small bombs from helicopters, placed by experts on skis or by the shooting of mortar or bazooka shells.

Another important area of our work consists of protecting areas with steel or wooden avalanche fences, erected to keep the snow in place. The same effect can

often be obtained by planting rows of trees and bushes in areas below the timberline where there's enough soil for them to grow.

We are even consulted by the Swiss Air Force, which won't let their fighter planes break the sound barrier if there's a chance that the supersonic boom created might cause an avalanche.

However, once an accident has happened, it is extremely important that a search and rescue party arrive as fast as possible, usually by helicopter, with all the necessary equipment to locate and dig out any victims. Today, small radio transmitters have been developed for skiers to carry and this makes it an easy task to locate them even under many meters of snow. Unfortunately, not everyone wears them, so the rescue organizations often have to resort to old fashioned search methods using long feeler-sticks and specially trained dogs.

Every morning, I take the funicular to the Institute. In winter, I bring my skis along and every evening I have a wonderful long run all the way down the mountain. It's an awful lot faster than using the funicular!

"Cheesemaking is a very precise process"

Ulrich Rentsch lives in Langnau with his wife and daughter. He is a true Swiss craftsman, the maker of one of Switzerland's most famous cheeses, Emmental.

I live at Langnau, which is about 35 km (20 miles) from the capital, Berne. Together with my wife, Christine, I run the town käserei, or dairy. Christine runs the store and I make the cheeses in the dairy. Christine has an assistant and I have an apprentice, they both live with us and we think of them as part of the family.

I am a fourth generation cheesemaker and this dairy has been run by my family since 1865. To become a cheesemaker I served three years as an apprentice and spent one year at dairy school. I also passed my master cheesemaker's exam, for which I was judged on the cheeses I made over a three-month period. Now I produce three Emmental cheeses every day. I am actually employed by the thirty-eight farmers in the district, who deliver the milk I need to make the cheese. There are two milk deliveries every day between 5:30 and 6:30 am and at the same hours in the

Ulrich uses a metal pulley to hoist the curd-filled cheesecloth from the vat.

Ulrich knocks on the maturing cheeses to see how far they have ripened.

evening. This means I work from 5:00 am to 6:30 pm seven days a week. The craft is dying because most qualified cheesemakers prefer to work the shorter hours in the cheese factory.

The farmers deliver about 3,000–4,000 liters (750–1,000 gallons) of milk daily and I use at least 90 percent to make the cheese. Cheesemaking is a very precise process. First the milk is poured into one of the vats, then I add exactly the right amount of rennet to make the curd form quickly. Certain other bacteria are added and the milk is stirred and heated to around 52°C (120°F). When the curd has formed, it is broken or cut up and lifted from the watery whey in a fine-mesh cheesecloth. I use a metal pulley for this as it weighs about 100 kilos (220 lb). Then I pack it into a wheel-shaped mold and salt it in strong brine. The curing and fermenting cheeses are stored in the cellar, which is divided into different rooms, all kept at different temperatures. The freshly made cheeses lie in large salt pans and other cheeses at different stages of ripening are stored on wooden shelves.

At the moment we do not own our home. We live above the käserei free of charge, that being part of our salary. One day we would like to buy a house. Our terms of employment are such that we receive a certain amount for running the käserei and the store and then we have to employ and pay whatever assistants we need. If we employed more people, we would have less money for ourselves so we work hard and think of our dream.

We will never be rich, but we are not poor either. Regine, our four-year-old daughter, goes to kindergarten three times a week. The kindergarten is not state run and we are glad that Regine was able to get a place. Often we are too busy to pay her much attention. I enjoy shooting and take part in as many competitions as possible. I am also a member of a yodeling choir. We try to get away for a vacation for two to three weeks every year. We usually go to the Costa Dorada in Spain where we can relax together as a family.

Facts

Capital City: Berne

Principle language: There are two principal languages in Switzerland: German and French. 73.5 percent of Swiss people are German-speaking, 20.1 percent speak French and come mainly from the southwest and west of Switzerland and only 4.1 percent of the population speak Italian; they are inhabitants of the south of Switzerland. A very small minority, in the east, speak Romansh. There are also many different dialects of each language, especially German, which vary in different regions.

Currency: 100 Rappen (centimes) = 1 Franken (Swiss Franc); 1.77 Franken = 1.00 US$ (June 1986).

Religion: Most Swiss people are Christians divided almost equally into 47.8 percent Protestant and 49.4 percent Catholic. 0.3 percent of the population are Jewish and there is a small minority of other religions.

Population: There are a total of 6,423,106 inhabitants of Switzerland (1983 figure), a rise from 6,269,783 in 1970. The average density of people per square kilometer is 155.5, and the land area is 41,293 square kilometers (15,943 square miles), which is about half the size of Maine. 65 percent of the population are of German descent, 18.4 percent French and 9.8 percent Italian. Switzerland's capital, Berne, has a population of 300,882 including the surrounding area, and Geneva's population is 371,677.

Climate: The climate in Switzerland is very varied, due to Switzerland's central position in Europe. It is open to the four main European air currents – from the Atlantic, the eastern continent, the northern subpolar region and the Mediterranean to the south. These air currents together with the sudden changes in relief from mountain to plateau cause many regional microclimates. Rainfall varies greatly from region to region too, except on the Central Plateau where the average rainfall is 10,000 mm per annum, average sunshine is 1,700 hours per annum and the average annual temperature is 7–9°C (44–48°F).

Government: Switzerland is a federation, which is split into 20 cantons and 6 half-cantons, each of which has its own constitution and laws. They are independently governed by the Council of States, which consists of 46 members (two for each canton, and one for each half-canton). These members are elected for three to four year periods at a time. The Federal State consists of the people, the cantons, the Federal Assembly (Parliament), the Federal Council (Government) and the Federal Tribunal. It is run by a president who is elected for a term of one year only, but who can be reelected in years to come for another one-year term. The federal government's duties are to ensure internal and external security and maintain diplomatic relations with foreign powers. Switzerland has always been recognized for its international neutrality since its origins, which date back to 1291. The Swiss did not take part in either of the World Wars and this is one of the main reasons why the United Nations was set up in Geneva in 1945 with the aim of promoting peace and diplomacy throughout the world. Switzerland is not a member but the membership is compiled from 159 different countries. Since 1959, government posts have been divided between the Social Democrats, the Radical Democrats, the Christian Democrats and the People's Party.

Housing: Due to Switzerland's wealth as a country and its small population, there are no housing problems. The style of houses vary greatly from region to region and as a whole, Switzerland is a very clean and tidy place. The architecture in German-speaking areas and large cities shows the stern efficiency of its people whereas in the west, especially Geneva, the houses are more graceful and picturesque. There are also many beautiful valley villages in the Alps.

Education: Each canton has its own system of education. The schools in each region have different sets of rules and regulations. Most children go to kindergarten for two years followed by elementary school, which is free and compulsory. At the end of elementary school they take a test to get into either secondary school, which lasts for three years, or a cantonal school, which lasts for six to seven years. After secondary school, children are issued with a school report and after cantonal school they take an exam called the Matura, which is set by the Swiss Federation and determines whether they will go to college or not. There are nine universities in Switzerland, all of which are fee-paying and very difficult to get into. The secondary schools are well attended and there are many private institutions as well as state run schools.

Agriculture: The primary agricultural pursuit is cattle raising for which Switzerland has become important throughout Europe. Income from dairying and cattle raising accounts for about half of all agricultural income. Because of the contour of the land large-scale crop growing is impossible and

Glossary

only accounts for half of the nation's demand. Two-thirds of farms combine grass and grain cultivation. The Valais, with its abundance of sunshine and artificial irrigation, concentrates on growing fruits, vegetables and berries.

Industry: Swiss precision engineering, especially in clocks and watches has long been famous although there is a steady decline for demand since cheaper products have been produced in Japan and Hong Kong. Heavy engineering, textiles, chocolate, chemicals and pharmaceuticals are all important export industries. Switzerland is a center of international banking and also draws considerable revenue from tourism both in the summer and winter, which accounts for some 15 percent of export income. The principal tourism attractions are the lakes, lake resorts and the mountains for activities including walking, mountaineering and winter sports. In 1983, Switzerland's receipts from tourism totaled 7,430 million Swiss francs.

Media: There are a large number of local newspapers in Switzerland because the country is divided into cantons. In 1983 there were 124 local newspapers in circulation. The *Blick* and the *Tages Anzeiger Zurich*, which are national newspapers, have the largest circulation followed by the *Neue Zurcher Zeitung, Berne Zeitung, Basler Zeitung* and the *24 Heures*. About 75 percent are printed in German, 20 percent in French and 5 percent in Italian. The two most respected dailies are *Neue Zurcher Zeitung* (est. 1780) and the French *Journal de Geneve* (est. about 1830). They both carry an exceptionally high proportion of foreign news and have a large readership abroad. There are 2,364,649 radio licenses and 2,082,578 television receivers in Switzerland (1983 figures). There are five medium-wave transmitters and twelve short-wave radio transmitters, including German, French and Italian channels. There are three television channels. A complete television program service for each linguistic region and regular broadcasts in Romansh are provided on the first channel. The second and third channels are used in each linguistic region for transmitting programs of the other two linguistic regions.

Alloy Mixture composed wholly or mainly of metals.

Bilingual Being fluent in two languages.

Canton Subdivision of a country.

Carding The process of untangling and straightening out natural fibers.

Catechism Religious instruction by question and answer.

Curd Coagulated substance formed by action of acids on milk.

Dialect A form of speech peculiar to a certain district.

Flora Plants of a region or environment.

Funicular Cable railway with ascending and descending cars counterbalanced.

Gauge The distance between a pair of rails or opposite wheels.

Hydrology The science of the properties of water.

Mass Roman Catholic celebration of the Eucharist.

Microclimate The climate of a small area.

Minerology The science of minerals.

Multinational company A company operating in several countries.

Rennet A milk clotting preparation from calf stomachs.

Whey The watery part of milk that remains liquid when the rest forms curds.

Acknowledgment

The publishers would like to thank the Swiss National Tourist office for supplying the pictures on pages 13, 17, 27, 35, 41; and UBS of Zurich for the picture on page 7.

Index